Hungry Vultures

A Play

Abdulai Walon-Jalloh

Sierra Leonean Writers Series

Hungry Vultures

ISBN: 978-99910-54-65-0

Sierra Leonean Writers Series

Foreword

Hungry Vultures is a satirical title which the playwright Abdulai Walon-Jalloh has given to his play. This is very intriguing to the reader who may want to know why the choice of title. Abdulai carefully brings out some of the contemporary issues with regards to family exploitation, politics, the quest for greener pasture and love.

The play opens with the preparation for the independence of a particular nation which has been under British rule. Being happy for independence, citizens have congregated outside the Colonial Administration Building chanting and it gets to the point where the police who are to control the crowd could not do so. When the crowd becomes rowdy, the British representatives have to run. This is followed by the jubilation and announcement of cabinet in Act One Scene Two.

By the time the reader gets to Act One Scene Three, the playwright introduces the market dues collector who is bent on collecting dues from traders. Ironically, all the dues collected are not judiciously used and Mama Kelleh being aware of such decides to dodge the dues collector. The issue of love is made manifest in the plot in Act One Scene One, this unity of action is seen among the jubilant crowd who are happy for the fact they are becoming independent. By the time the reader gets to Act Two Scene One, the love is also manifested as Paul's Rendezvous is also used as a meeting point for most of the citizens in the working class in spite of this kind of love which the playwright portrays; there is the issue of class distinction. One striking example of class distinction is the love between Borbor Kelleh and Tamatfa who is Mr. Cole's daughter. Borbor Kelleh, who hails from a humble background is not considered as fit to be the lover of Tamatfa and as such is intimidated. In the end, Tamatfa has to abandon the child she has with Borbor Kelleh and is sent overseas to fend for herself. Ironically Tamatfa who is from an affluent family back home has everything at her beck and call, is found in a difficult situation abroad to the extent that she has to resort to doing menial jobs in order to survive. This also points out the cultural shock which most people (especially Africans) encounter when they leave for the West, as it is not all the time rosy.

In another development, Pa Morlai, in Act Two Scene Two, reveals his plan to forcefully take his family to the city to live with Mama Kelleh's family even when his son asks whether he has consulted Mama Kelleh and family. For Papa Morlai, it is useless to inform the sister he has raised and moving to the city to leave with his sister would cause no harm. This also brings out another issue prevalent in most traditional settings; even though Pa Morlai and family have everything in the village they live in, he is still not content because better life exists in the city. This is a sheer case of blind greed or wanton exploitation. He is shocked to note that what he has expected does not turn out well and as such decides to return to the village with his family.

Walon-Jalloh is commended for his efforts as this play is his debut into the drama genre of literature.

Prince E. A. J. Kenny
Head of Department
Department of Language Studies
Fourah Bay College University Sierra Leone

Endorsements

1)

Hungry Vultures by Walon-Jalloh is an attempt to trace the development of a people through several decades. The play comes to life at the dawn of independence and terminates during a football match and in between the lives of three generations have been laid bare for all to see, love, hate and empathize with. The play's fabric is replete with love (Tamatfa and Borbor Kelleh), exploitation (the Morlai Family's trip to the city to live with the Kelly Family amongst others), revenge (Borbor Kelleh's anger at his uncle's treatment of his mother after the demise of Papa Kelleh thus one of the reasons for joining the army), realization (Papa Morlai realising his mistake of coming to the city to live with his sister and thus returning to the village to the happiness of Mamady), loss (the death of Papa Kelleh and Borbor Morlai), corruption (food supplies diverted to the market away from their intended purpose), unexplained wealth (the Cole scenario), dignified labour (the Porter at Tamatfa's apartment abroad), political patronage (the Mayor and Papa Kelleh), hope and regeneration (joy and warmth lavished on Junior Kelly) and political disturbances in the forms of coups and rebel war. The playwright skilfully picks his way through the many tunnels, characters and events and time spans to a logical conclusion where everyone is at least settled though the reader is left with so many unanswered questions such as the source of Cole's wealth, how did Tamatfa's transition come about? How did Borbor Morlai and Papa Kelly die?

I will boldly recommend that everyone, Sierra Leoneans in particular, read this light but serious debut play by Abdulai Walon-Jalloh.

Dr. Leopold Foullah
Dean Faculty of Arts
Fourah Bay College, USL

2)

Hungry Vultures is a must-read play written with the intent to prick the conscience of Sierra Leoneans. The play takes us down memory lane, to the days of colonialism, independence, post- independence and roots us firmly in the present.

Abdulai Walon-Jalloh's lenses focus not only on the political arena, but also on issues such as the man-woman relationship, love, marriage, the family unit, corruption, morality, the position of women, etc.

The lives of the masses are seen against the background of the political landscape of divisory politics, attempted coups and usurpation of power. With the subtlety of a poet, Walon- Jalloh hints at the excitement and expectations of the masses now that they have achieved independence. But the political landscape is fraught with problems; it is either one party fighting the other, the military usurping power or the rebels attempting to snatch power. The losers are obviously the masses. They suffer or die as soldiers, innocent citizens or infiltrators.

Walon-Jalloh does not seek to write a wholly political play. He intends to raise the alarm, to remind us about what we have forgotten and emphasize the point that we should not go down certain roads in our country's history. Not ever again.

Walon-Jalloh puts the masses under a microscope as they endeavour to make sense of their lives in an apparently senseless and changing world. In this play, Pa

Kelleh the dreamer (not another Joseph; Joseph dreams about the future, but Pa Kelleh dreams about the past) is left with empty hands in spite of his support of the mayor and his political party (something tells me that he died of a broken heart).

There is also condemnation of some of the customs of Sierra Leoneans, especially those that victimize women. Uncle Kelleh inherits Mama Kelleh and abuses her physically, verbally and psychologically. His attitude reveals that he has no place in this century, and the dramatist castigates him and men of his stamp for abusing and oppressing women and children.

Similarly, as the play progresses, the impression is created that the dramatist has a spy in every household. The high-handed way in which Pa Morlai relates to his wife and the initial problem in the home of Borbor Kelleh and Tamatfa reflect and capture the relationship between husbands and wives in a good number of homes.

The darkness of the human heart and the issue of greed are underpinned in this play by the pregnant title of one of the newspapers thus: 'Supplies meant for the vulnerable find their way to the market stalls'. This is not a strange or new phenomenon in Africa and is an index of the pervasive corruption in Sierra Leone in particular. Of course, Walon-Jalloh cannot avoid writing about the issue of malice or man's inhumanity to man. Sierra Leoneans agree that most of the atrocities committed against them during the country's civil war were committed by their acquaintances. Houses were looted and burnt down by those that knew the inhabitants and women were raped by their acquaintances. Thus in this play, Borbor Kelleh and Feroz become soldiers in order to 'even up'.

The dramatist subtly draws attention to the moral bankruptcy of the people, citing the issue of married men frequenting Paul's Rendezvous, in the red light district.

It needs to be said that there are certain instances in which the play leaves us in the dark. We do not really know what happened to Cole, the diamond smuggler at the end of the play. There is a hint that he also smuggles something else. Drugs perhaps?

One would have loved to have a clear idea of time in the play. It would have helped for us to know something about the passage of time from one scene or act to the other.

In a similar vein, though the value of true love is upheld in the Borbor Kelleh-Tamatfa relationship (after their quarrel, separation and reconciliation) the dramatist should have suggested how they overcame the class barrier.

What I also hold against the dramatist is the fact that Mama Kelleh and Mama Morlai do not seem to have individual identities of their own. Walon-Jalloh should give them their own individual names. This is the 21st Century!

When the play draws to a close, we are still left with some urgent questions. Are the hungry vultures the politicians or infiltrators who are always looking for opportunities to usurp power? Are they caterpillars like Cole, who once lived in a 'two roomed affair' with no money to his name, but now lives in a mansion, with a 'huge solid gate' and lots of cars? Or, are they the masses, who are also out there to exploit others and get rich quickly.

Whoever the vultures are, **Hungry Vultures** is a topical play that, as it were, holds a mirror to Sierra Leone. It touches on her political life and highlights some topical concerns. And as one turns the final page of the play it becomes apparent that Walon-Jalloh is saying in so many words, 'he who has ears let him hear'.

Elizabeth Lucy Kamara
Head of English Language Unit
Department of Language Studies
Fourah Bay College, USL.

3)

Hungry Vultures by the playwright Abdulai Walon Jalloh is a tumultuous, anxious, didactic and captivating genre - triangulated play. The play equilibrates the perspective of Africa in general and Sierra Leone in particular, state collapse with thrilling sensation of national power, social charisma and state authority in a distance and lock of mysticism and philosophical ideals based on cultural inclinations and overutilization of it embedded in the mind of the reader. However, lodged in confused family drama, poverty and suspicion with a little bit of up-stream romance and the interloping of the old ways of inertia due to colonialism trailed to contemporary paths of wanting national progress and the interjection of lust tales diffused into that current of unfounded hope, **Hungry Vultures** grossly is character - driven and almost all the suspense comes from the characters. What will unfold next and how will it be put keeps the reader on the edge. The interstices of the scenes keep one from endless suspense and a surgical dramatic enclave of stylized Sierra Leonean characterization to the coveted spot; that is the consciousness and insight of the playwright.

The caveat for this is that Borbor Kelleh is a moderately enchanting, courageous and ambitious protagonist but lacks the inner temerity to greatness as he allows, initially, Tamatfa to slip away. He is both similar to and at the same time, utterly different from a typical 'Freetong' urban teenage boy. From the play's inception

Tamatfa reveals a sense of mystery, not just to the reader, but also to herself. One is forced to ask whether her love stems truly from teenage melodrama or the lack of the required opportunity to catch the glimpse of her heart that upstages her being. Is her place the rightful pedestal for Borbor Kelleh? This pinning question dwarfed the thought of Borbor Kelleh and a felting sting of my literary taste buds bracing the sleeping urges to keep me leafing through the seeming scenes that kept me to the end.

The characterization in the play creates a Sierra Leonean connection that depicts the assuming reality of what unfolds from independence, to post and the fear that gripped the conscience of the country during military regimes and individual sacrifices, during the civil war, consumed to save the nation as Borbor Kelleh had no option but to join the military, a decision he kept discreet. This felt very real to me. The characters too are compelling and sometimes intimidating, but most of the time, I could understand what has infuriated them and I also understand why Pa Kelleh's attitude is so bizarre with his own wife and son. Critically, I may be cajoled to only pick on the scenes which denotes and resonates something about the play's revolving themes, to such a degree that when the characters are taken away, this sometimes felt fictional, though as characters they themselves stand together in this comedy.

Arguably, one of the overwhelming highlights of this play was the issue of ideological warfare and language. The writing is lucid, sparing and direct, but at the same time, stunningly accurate at conjuring an ominous aura of peril, daunting and joyous circumstance, a disturbing, eerie impression. Sufficiently, at any moment I picked up the play I had to smile coyly but better still drifted, while every break I took from reading made me think about Tamatfa and cringe at what she might become and what might happen to her love affair. The play ends with a note of comfort, hope, emotion, unity and aspiration that I am in a dilemma of serenity to give meanings, because it raises almost as many questions as it answers. Suffice it to say that I doff my heart with the iconic perspective with which the **Hungry Vulture's** curtain comes down and I will certainly be reading more of Walon-Jalloh's works in his stalwart gift to the literary domain.

Mohamed Bangura
Lecturer, Department of Sociology and Social Work
Departmental Examination Coordinator
Secretary General Academic Staff Association (ASA)
Fourah Bay College, University of Sierra Leone

4)

The play **Hungry Vultures** is set in a fictional country that resonates with Sierra Leone, a West African nation. The story spans three decades in the lives of people torn apart by profound changes. On the whole the play projects too many sub-themes and there is the seeming challenge of blending the themes of love, corruption, societal injustice and inequality in family life which in themselves on the other hand represent the vibrancy of the human condition.

Teddy Foday Musa
Lecturer Department of Peace and Conflicts Fourah Bay College, USL

5)

The play **Hungry Vultures** written by Abdulai Walon-Jalloh largely encapsulates a diachronic presentation of a political satire which spans from colonial era to present day; perhaps, which aptly mirrors Sierra Leone as a third world country in the West African sub region of the wider African continent.

The play opens with country's attainment of independence from her colonial master, after a stern agitation. In the interim, the sly nature and character of the police force – serving the newly-independent government as it diligently served the defunct colonial hegemony came to the fore – quite a mirthful behaviour noted in Act One Scenes One and Two.

The independent government and country is in a bad shape, riddled by poverty, corruption and bad governance punctuated by series of military coups and an insurrection. However, there are also instances of love (Tamatfa and Borbor Kelleh), family exploitation and blind greed as exhibited by Pa Morlai in the play.

The mention of the families of Pa Sesay and Pa Morlai toiling in the farms in Act One Scene Five, business having gone bad at the night club, with opposite love birds and rivals displaying tensions in Act One Scene One; with Pa Morlai and family living in a hut – "sleeping on a bench-cum-bed"; and the issue of hunger in Act Three Scenes Two and Four, as well as parents not being able to pay school fees for their children in Act Three Scene Four are all indicators of poverty and the appalling life which citizens live.

The case of Pa Kelleh returning from work and not sure of going back to his work because of his failure to rally support for the party (as noted in Act Two Scenes Two and Three); the expressed doubt over the issue of free education pronounced by the government in Act Three Scene Four to mention but a few are indicators of palpable corruption.

Moreover, the issue of non-regular payment of salaries to workers, arbitrary arrest and detention of citizens mentioned in Act Three Scene Three; Mr. Bomti, the teacher, saying: "our beloved nation has been characterized by chaos because our leaders have ushered in a new era that will rid this nation of party multiplicity," in Act Four Scene One; and Feroz saying that; " from the inside, the leader want to pass over the baton and thus deems it wise to have new blood in the nation's army to foil the aspirations of older contenders" (Act Four Scene Four) are matters of bad governance.

Next, the proposal by Mama Kelleh to slaughter a sheep in order to appease the spirits for the failure of her son, Borbor Kelleh; the mention of fetish being responsible for the sacking of her husband (Pa Kelleh) from job, with the proposal to let her brother prepare some "powerful medicine" for her family, all in Act Two Scene Four are cases of superstition typical of African values.

16

Above all there is an issue of love between Tamatfa and Borbor Kelleh in Act Five Scene Two where the former says: "I'm sorry for my parents' behaviour. You know I love you." Furthermore, Tamatfa in Act Six Scene Two expresses remorse: "I'm sorry ... I was foolish and spoilt ...". These are expressions of love, though the parents of the two parties did not approve of the relationship. It implies that even in the thick of poverty and hardship, love is imminent. Not even hate could prevent it.

In any case, the entire ensemble is carefully choreographed, making it incredibly illuminating with an apt description of characters, scenes and scenarios. However, the title **Hungry Vultures** may appear a bit absurd being that it is not reflective of the story. Nonetheless, the title represents the veiled indictment of us as humans with all our foibles and foolishness in the form of blind quest, naked greed and wanton exploitation of the already exploited. At the same time, the three decade-span for the story seems untenable since the time is relatively short; otherwise half a century would sound more appropriate and realistic. But again this unrealistic time frame is what makes it a work of fiction and not the already known history of Sierra Leone. Finally, the mention of vultures buffeting the sky really lacks any place in the story but yet again, who would not want to dabble in symbolism and parallel manifestations of characters' states of mind and conditions via external objects in order to add colour to the drama.

Notwithstanding, the effort of the playwright is laudable and this play is a must-read.

Issa Roberts
Lecturer of Linguistics
Department of Language Studies
Fourah Bay College University of Sierra Leone

The Play

Hungry Vultures

List of Characters

- **Leader** of the newly-independent nation
- **Old Man** at State House
- **Police** at State House
- **Mrs. and Mr. Stooke- Married couple** working in the Colonial Administration
- **Mrs and Mr. Sloane**- Married couple working in the Colonial Administration
- **Messenger** in Colonial Administration
- **Due Collector** at the Market
- **Mama Kelleh and Papa Kelleh**- Married couple living in the City
- **Borbor Kelleh** son of the Kelleh Family
- **Junior Kelleh** is the son of Borbor Kelleh and Tamatfa
- **Amadu** is Borbor Kelleh's classmate
- **Mr. Quicksilver** teacher at the school
- **Bellcamp** is the landlord of Papa and Mama Kelleh.
- **The Sesay's** are the Morlai's neighbours in the village
- **Mama Morlai and Pa Morlai** are married couple living in the village
- **Borbor Morlai** is the son of the Morlai's
- **Mamady** is the sister of Borbor Morlai
- **Paul** is the owner of Paul's Rendezvous a nightclub in the City

- **Attendant** at Paul's Rendezvous
- **Santigie** a frequenter of Paul's Rendezvous
- **Mr. Boima** a civil servant is a frequenter of Paul's Rendezvous
- **Mr. Cole** is also another frequenter of the club and father of Tamatfa
- **Fatalie** is the wife of Mr. Cole
- **Tamatfa** is the daughter of Mr. Cole and Fatalie
- **Radio Announcer**
- **Mayor** of the Council
- **Speaker** of the Parliament
- **Honourable Lonka and Honourable Juma** in the House of Parliament
- **Jay** the owner of Jay's Common Hunt
- **Feroz** a friend of Borbor Kelleh and frequenter of Jay's Common Hunt
- **Stranger** informs Boima about the rebels
- **Vendor** of Dailies
- **Porter** at Tamatfa's residence abroad
- **Restaurant Boss**
- **Customers**
- **Mr. Bomti** a teacher

ACT ONE SCENE 1

AFTERNOON

COLONIAL ADMINISTRATION BUILDING

The skies are clear and an irate but subdued crowd gather outside the colonial administration headquarter in Liberty Town chanting slogan and displaying messages on placards, banners and floor mats. Colony police are pushing the steady crowd back while insults and greetings are being traded from one side to the other. Inside the building white and black colonial officials are shifting restlessly in their seats as if ready to jump out of their skins in case the crowd outside were to overpower the Colonial Police.

Mr. Stooke: [Sweating profusely and batting flies with the incessant wave of his hands]
            I wish this braying could stop! Couldn't they use some other medium?

Mrs. Sloane: [Unperturbed by the turmoil outside for her mind   is   elsewhere].   They   have every right to. This is their country by the way we repelled the French in the eleventh century

Mr. Sloane: [Ignoring his wife's comments]
            They must prepare themselves first before demanding the right of self-determination. I think Her Majesty must protect the Crown.

Mrs. Stooke: [Infuriated by the incessant drumming].
For how long, Slo…?

Mrs. Sloane: [Eyeing Mr. Stooke with all the venom in
her eyes]. Two minutes.

Mr. Sloane: [Exploded]. Your views are not sought.

Mrs. Sloane: [Eyes flashing and voice lisping] Might as
well not.

[Messenger rushes in breathlessly]

Mr. Stooke: [Quickly]. Have they broken loose?

Messenger: [Resignedly] Yes, sir!

Mr. Sloane, Mrs Sloane and Mr. Stooke flee in all
directions. Messenger stands in astonishment not
knowing what to do. He sits on the floor and helps
himself with the untouched lunch. In the distance, the
muted cries of the crowd fade away.

ACT ONE SCENE 2

MORNING

STATE AVENUE

Post-independence celebrations linger on. At State Avenue, the leader announces his cabinet. The small crowd consisting of relatives of would- be appointees gather around State House to listen to the State Address hoping to hear the names of their relatives. Nearby, cultural display of every kind, executed with such dexterity and determination as if their lives depended on it, go on ablaze.

Leader: [Desperately trying to control his superfluous garment in order to make it fit the small frame that is carrying it]. Hm! Hm! Free at last! Free at last! My people it was not easy. Our opposite numbers at Whitehall were reluctant to grant us the right to determine our own destinies…they said we were in a hurry and incompetent to handle matters of grave concern…we proved them wrong. Today I am forming a new cabinet from our own kind. Mr…. [Applause starts only to be followed by a deafening applause when a close relative's name is announced]

Police: [Anxious not to be found wanting]. Move! Move back! Move! Are you deaf and blind? Can't you hear me? Can't you see the line? [Starts beating the crowd back with controlled blows from his truncheon].

24

Old Man: [Pleadingly]. This is State House and we mean no harm. Show some respect I have been to two world wars …. In the first war I was a cook and in the second I actually killed people in uniform like you.

Police: [Stunned]. You mean you will kill me ?

Old Man: [Confidently but jokingly]. Possibly, …

Police: [Looks around for help but could not find any because his colleagues are far away fending off the sun] but this is not a war.

Old Man: [Menacingly]. And why would you want to provoke one? [Drumming continues]

ACT ONE SCENE 3

EVENING

MARKET

Market is showing signs of lethargy save for the quarrel that has lasted for four hours between the Dues Collector and Mama Kelleh.

Dues Collector: [Determinedly] Mama Kelleh you will have to pay your dues today. I shall have none of your usual excuses of not selling a tie of cassava leaves.

Mama Kelleh: [Exhausted by the marathon haggling with her adversary] Please come tomorrow! The money you saw me counting belongs to the Thrift Collector.

Dues Collector: [Re-energised]. Does he build you public latrines?

Mama Kelleh: [Warms up to the counter-attack]. He keeps my money for a minimal fee.

Dues Collector: [Transfers his money bag to one side]. I am charging you with…

Mama Kelleh: [Fuming] … what?

Dues Collector: [Beaming]. Refusal to pay market dues to Council Authority.

Mama Kelleh: [Resignedly. Here…take the money and don't come here for two weeks.

Dues Collector: [Stretches both hands and his mouth exploding rows of muddy teeth reluctantly hiding behind gullied lips]. Thank you!

Mama Kelleh: [Hurriedly rewraps her lappa for the ninety second time that day before flashing her eyes for Kelleh] Kelleh? Kelleh?

Borbor Kelleh: [From under the stall] Hm! Hm! Ahh! I am here. When are we going home ? I am hungry.

Mama Kelleh: [Mockingly feigning anger] Come out you fool with a head like your father's

Borbor Kelleh: [Teasingly]. Ask for a divorce.

Mama Kelleh: [Laughs]. No one will pick him up if I dump him. I'm a sympathetic woman you know   …..
Have you collected the palm oil?

Borbor Kelleh: [On arriving] I want to have a step mother…..

Mama Kelleh: [Jealous]. Keep quiet!   Answer my question.

Borbor Kelleh: [Subdued]. Yes.

Mama Kelleh: [Laughing]. Let's hurry home and cook the meal before your father returns from work. [Exit]

ACT ONE SCENE 4

MORNING

SCHOOL

At school Borbor Kelleh derides Amadu for sleeping in class. Teacher stands in front of the class thundering excuses why he cannot teach that morning. He is out of sorts.

Borbor Kelleh: [Protruding tongue at Amadu for Neneh to see] Amadu the sleeping champion. What did you eat yesterday before coming to school? A house?

Amadu: [Not liking it]. Yes!

Borbor Kelleh: [Excited].Whose house?

Amadu: [Elated]. Your house [Class burst out laughing]

Borbor Kelleh: [Sensing defeat]. Did you have enough?

Amadu: [Triumphantly]. That was why I slept.

[Laughing becomes wild. Bell rings]

[Enters Mr. Quicksilver]

[Class quiet again]

Mr. Quicksilver: [Shifting from one foot to the other]. Hm! Hm! Hm! Silence of the graveyard.

[Disturbing quiet ensued]. My wife put too much pepper in the soup yesterday. And I have a running nose [sneezes]. I can't teach like this [coughing and sneezing whilst class attempt to laugh]...ill-advised! Hold it right there lest you carry Everest on your backsides ... Hm ... Hm ... Hm. Bow! In fact, sleep until I tell you not to.... [Bell rings and Mr. Quicksilver hurries out].

ACT ONE SCENE 5

AFTERNOON

VILLAGE FARM

The Sesay's are hard at work on their farm and also contemplating moving to the city to Mama Kelleh's residence.

Pa Morlai: [knee deep in the swamp preparing it for the next planting season. The city will offer us more.

[Some other parts of the forest]

Mama Morlai: [Carrying a bundle of dried sticks on her head. And in one hand a bucket filled with cassava tubers. The other hand is dragging along her reluctant and spoiled daughter-Mamady] Mama Kelleh has forgotten about us. We are going to meet her in the city. When one puts on a hat she expects her height to increase. Freetown we are coming … hurry you lazy fool!

Mamady: [Grudgingly]. My foot!

Mama Morlai: [Stops]. What about your foot?

Mamady: [Feigning]. It hurts badly

Mama Morlai: [Angry but pleased]. Come here… [Grabs her quickly before continuing her long trek home]

[Some other parts of the forest]

Borbor Morlai: [lying on his back dreaming about beautiful girls and a never ending feast of jollof rice….suddenly wakes up] I have not caught anything today. Father will have my skin today. How about this dead squirrel for supper? ….. [Picks it up hurriedly and moves on] I wonder what Borbor Kelleh is doing this moment? Listening to the radio? Or beckoning to girls under the full view of street-lights….or eating jollof rice…yes that is it….[Raises his head to the sky and arms spread out]Kelleh keep some for us for we are coming. [Runs].

ACT TWO SCENE 1

EVENING

NIGHTCLUB

Paul's Rendez-vous throbs, with the usual frequenters. Attendants are alert and responsive to every beckoning by customers. Music blazes out in a rather subdued manner so as not to swallow the livid conversations of acolytes. Paul is tense and worried for business is lean and the commercial sex workers' arrival has not helped matters either.

Santigie: [slurring] P-a-u-l ... P-a-u-l ... Hurry ... two pints! ... Please!

Attendant: [Anxious] Money please! Beer, after.

Santigie: [Angry] Get me your boss before I crush your brighter grammar legs. Have you seen your legs? They resemble those of the men, in the Brighter Grammar, carrying verbs and nouns on their heads.

Attendant: [Confused]. I might be of help.

[Enters Mr Boima]

Santigie: [Sobering up]. Mr. Boima is there anything I could do for you?

Mr. Boima: [Solemnly]. Into your skin fool!!

Santigie: [Failingly]. I tho-ught you would do fine with an ash-tray.

Mr. Boima: [Smiles]. This is not the office and there are capable hands here, after all.

[Enters Mr Cole]

Mr. Cole: [Noisily]. Paul! Paul! Paul! Three pints of beer, please.

Santigie: [Disturbed]. On whose account?

Mr. Cole: [Grinning]. Mine of course.

Mr. Boima: [Eyes flashing]. Santigie! Enough of that, scram!

Santigie: [Confidently]. You know you don't really mean that......Hm! hm!hm!......the other part of the affair. [Closes his right eye]

Mr. Boima: [Understandingly]. Be rather than heard.... [Turns to Mr. Cole] I don't like it.

Mr. Cole: [Stunned]. Did I do anything?

Mr. Boima: [Laughs]. Not you. It is the authorities. They have arrogated all the powers to themselves. I sit all day in the office not implementing anything.

Mr. Cole: [Amused]. Better to sit and do nothing. I like idling around. It means we have more time to ourselves and that's wonderful.

Mr. Boima: [Astounded]. You can't think, scum. They may decide not to pay our salaries at all. You know what that means? No more rounds of beer buying.

Mr. Cole: [Shrinks]. I think you are exaggerating.... Beer please...how do you know about this?

Mr. Boima: [Hurriedly]. They sent a dispatch this morning ordering senior council authority to send on leave most of our junior workers.... and worse still without pay.

Mr. Cole: [Agape]. Are you carrying out the order?

Mr. Boima: [Resignedly]. They have threatened me with an official enquiry regarding my handling of council funds in the event I refuse to act accordingly.

Mr. Cole: [Shaking his head]. No wonder we are now free of pressure from within, how would they govern us?

Mr. Boima: [Head in both palms]. From the centre.

[Paul enters]

Paul: [Concerned]. What is happening? Are new records not going to be set today? You are eight pints short of the standing record.

[Boima, Cole and Santigie look up at Paul with flashing and devouring rage. Mr. Cole places the money on the table and they all storm out of the bar leaving Paul wondering whether he has said something amiss...]

[Lights fade]

ACT TWO SCENE 2

VILLAGE

NIGHT

Outside the Morlai family's paternal hut, Pa Morlai is stretched out on his wooden bench-cum-bed warding off recalcitrant nocturnal insects that are rather hard at it before their usual time at midnight. He inadvertently aims an elephant blow at a fly that has come to rest on his right jaw. As the Hercules blow lands the fly moves away causing the uncontrolled blow to land on Pa Morlai's right jaw. He winces, grates his teeth and shoots up erect as if nothing has happened. The sound of the blow attracts the attentive ears of Mama Morlai who is preparing the evening meal of boiled cassava and bush meat. The moon is up, the zephyr is rustling the leaves around the compound and a characteristic stillness pervades the outer confines of the neighbouring forests.

Mama Morlai: [Turning]. What is it? Pa Morlai are you alright?

Pa Morlai: [Bemused]. I am hungry and you are killing me by making me talk.

[Enters Borbor Morlai]

Borbor Morlai: [Panting]. Someone is stealing from our farm.

Pa Morlai and Mama Morlai: [In unison]. What?

Borbor Morlai: [Confidently] Didn't you hear the sound of a falling coconut?

34

Pa Morlai: [Smarting from the blow] You too are hungry. Tell Mama Morlai to finish up this cooking. In fact you Borbor you've killed me because I've talked for the second time and without food either.....where is Mamady?

Mama Morlai: [Putting the pot down]. She is sleeping.

Pa Morlai: [Worried]. What did you feed her?

Mama Morlai: [Surprised]. Nothing, can't you see I'm only preparing food now.

Pa Morlai: [Feigning sternness]. Borbor, wake her up. An overloaded stomach facilitates activities in the night thereby not displeasing the spirits that would be playing with one's tummy.

[Returns to the bench]

Mammady: [Rubbing the left eye with the back of the left hand]. I want to sleep. Leave me alone. I'm not hungry.

Mama Morlai: [Overjoyed but pretends not to be]. Shut up! Fool! Over here. Papa is over there and he does not want to be disturbed.

Mammady: [Notices the outstretched figure on the wooden bench]. Oh!

Borbor Morlai: [Chuckles]. Ought to have shown some respect to me first. I'm papa's carbon copy. Mind that.

[Places both hands to the side of his face, eyes popped out and tongue hanging out limply]

Mammady: [Cringes and inches closer to Mama Morlai]. Mama tell him to stop because I don't like it.

[Mama Morlai dishes and calls on Papa Morlai to come closer in order to set off the evening feast.]

Pa Morlai: [Swallows hard after dumping a football-size handful into his mouth to the admiration of Borbor Morlai and consternation of Mammady and Mama Morlai] I have thought about it. We are moving to the city to Mama Kelleh.

Borbor Morlai: [Unable to suppress his relief after all]. Have you talked to Mama Kelleh about It?

Pa Morlai: [Arrogantly]. She is my sister. I brought her up with my own hands. By the way, she need not be consulted... tuk ... tuk ...tuk... It has never been that way in our family.

Mamady: [Perturbed] Hm...what about our sheep, fowls, goats, the houses and the farm....don't they need loo ...?

Pa Morlai: [swiftly with the anger of the river god] Keep quiet and eat your food. When did you learn to speak in my presence. So Mama Morlai you've taught your child how to undermine my authority in this house eh ?

Mama Morlai: [Hesitantly]. Please don't s-t-a-r-t it now f-o-r the sake of peace.

[They eat in silence]

ACT TWO SCENE 3

CITY

NIGHT

Pa Kelleh has returned home from work with the possibility of never returning to work at the council headquarters. In bed pondering what has gone wrong, he sleeps off only to be reliving the stalemate of 1967. He was a firebrand of the party in those days and they had promised him a life-time job at council if he were to galvanise support for the party that was yet to taste power.

Mayor: [Sternly]. Look here Kelleh if you maximize output here in our favour the sky is the limit. This is from the Pa himself. You have his word.

Kelleh: [Confused]. What should I do? The other side is strong and is getting stronger every day.

Mayor: [Impatient]. Create distractions. Get someone to holler in the middle of the night with the cries of help! Help! Help! They are taking me away!

Kelleh: [Surprised]. Just that. That is easy.

Mayor: [Warming up to the task by confounding his colleague with the newest tricks on divisory politics of throwing sand in the eyes of your opponent.] Kill a fowl in the middle of the night and spill its blood in the door-way of our opponent's supporters and get someone to do the cry of being carted away.

Kelleh: [Awed]. Where did you learn these techniques from?

Mayor: [Push his chest forward]. Somewhere [Pointing to the northern part of the sky]. Over there.

Kelleh: [Astounded]. You mean in the sky.

Mayor: [Laughs] Do it tonight and I'll take you to see the Pa and have you recount your exploits in his presence.

[Borbor Kelleh enters noisily and inadvertently wakes up Papa Kelleh]

Pa Kelleh: [Opens his eyes and sees Borbor Kelleh]. Get me your mother. Both of you should come. I've something to tell you.

Borbor Kelleh: [Surprised]. Papa I am very sorry for rudely waking you up. Please I don't mean it. You know mama will punish me for being unmindful.

Pa Kelleh: [Looks at his son]. I said go and get me your mother it is something worse than that. And go now.

[Borbor rushes out calling 'Mama']

ACT TWO SCENE 4

CITY

NIGHT

Mama Kelleh rushes in panting and struggling to cover her body with the scanty cloth she can find. Borbor Kelleh on seeing his mother dives to the floor to avoid the semi nudity of his mother. Mama Kelleh finds him lying face down on the matless floor.

Mama Kelleh: [Almost dying for wants of air]. Oh! My son is dead. They've killed him. I said it. Let's have some water. A sheep will be slaughtered tomorrow to ward off their evil glances. It is because you've been promoted to class three. I see.

Borbor Kelleh: [Eyes fast closed, points to papa's room] Papa is calling you and me as well.

[They move into the other room]

Papa Kelleh: [Sombrely]. They've retrenched me. I can't go back to work.

Mama Kelleh: [Almost fainting but rallies her spirits] After causing my son to, almost go blind they final got my husband. I shall fight them to the end. [Waves her fist]. I shall get my brother to prepare some powerful medicine for this family. Pa Morlai, diviner of the unknown master of darkness and king of the seas, your sister is distraught oh! Please come and rescue us!

[Mama Kelleh and Borbor Kelleh leave. Papa Kelleh relapses into another fitful sleep]

Mayor: [Disturbed]. There was a stalemate Kelleh. The situation is confusing.

Kelleh: [Slightly undisturbed]. Is it why the men in uniform are holding on to the seat of power... eh what about taking me to see the Pa?

Mayor: [Dumbfounded]. The Pa has fled.

Kelleh: [Unperturbed] When is he coming back?

Mayor: [Realises the shallowness of Kelleh]. Soon.

Kelleh: How soon?

Mayor: Very soon...

[Mama Kelleh re-enters to look for her ju-ju things from under the bed in the event   wakes up Pa Kelleh]

Mama Kelleh: [Reassuringly]. Just sleep like a baby your warrior will do the fighting for the Kelleh family.

[Searches and Pa Kelleh relapses into yet another dream]

Mayor: [Elatedly]. The Pa has been installed. Now Kelleh you'll have to see him. But we will have to plan it, for it takes time and protocol to see him even me of all people.

Kelleh: [Takes solace in that]. O.K!

Mayor: [Confidently]. Haven't you heard?

Kelleh: [Stonily]. About what?

Mayor: [Gloating]. You're to go to council headquarters and get your confirmation of job-for-life.

Kelleh: [Falls to ground]. You can't be serious!

Mayor: [Waxes confidently]. But am I not?

Kelleh: [Squares up]. You, indeed, are!

[Cock crows in the distance]

ACT TWO SCENE 5

CITY

MORNING

The Morlai family, just arrived from up country, deployed their possessions in the Kelleh's household to the chagrin of Pa Kelleh and the fulfilment of Mama Kelleh's dream. She uses her principal to pay off the travelling costs of the Morlai family to the city.

Mama Morlai: [Effusively]. How is the city? I hope it is doing you fine?

Mama Kelleh: [Buoyantly]. It is a better place to live now than before.

Mammady: [Smiles]. Aunty Kelleh, where is Borbor?

Mama Kelleh: [Responding immediately but also covering the supposedly horrifying debacles that have befallen the family]. Out partying with a friend whose father assured us that Kelleh would be well looked after.

Pa Kelleh: [Bursts out laughing]. Hello everybody. Am I missing anything here:- Pa Morlai, Mama Morlai, Borbor Morlai and Mamady welcome to our nest. Have you washed and eaten? By the way, how is everyone out there? I hope they are all doing fine?-Mama Kelleh [whispers in her ear] ask Pa Bah to extend my credit facility: bring bread, ten loaves, butter, sugar, sardines [speaks loudly for everyone to hear.]Tell him I shall not have any of his excuses. I need my money now ok…

Mama Kelleh: [Looks up wide-eyed]. Yes Pa Kelleh it shall be done.

Pa Morlai: [Nudges at the side of Mama Morlai and whispers into her ears]. Didn't I tell you that coming to the city will solve our problems? No more toiling in the farm [He acknowledges to himself].

Borbor Morlai: [Joyously] Uncle Kelleh thank you very much.
[They all disperse].

ACT THREE SCENE 1

CITY

PARLIAMENT

MORNING

The Honourable Speaker rushes into Parliament Building leaving parliamentarians wondering what has happened that would have caused the unprecedented whirlwind entry of the Honourable Speaker. Is the new leader dead? Or has any of the world powers given the thumbs up sign to the happening that is about to befall and eclipse the nation? In any case most think it prudent to follow after him and ask questions later. The parliamentarians are buoyant and overtly optimistic for they are about to witness, in fact, change an age-old tradition in their history of their budding but fledgling state. 'Nation' yes but 'State' not yet. Or until after today.

Speaker: [Solemnly] by the powers vested in me and in accordance with Parliamentary Order ... I declare this session open and that all Parliamentary Procedures remain in force and any breach of the aforesaid is proscribed. Good morning ... this morning we have the supreme task to forge a novel identity for our beloved nation whose statehood still hangs in the balance. I say this because matters of grave concern like finance, defence et al have to be dictated by someone from without ... this must end and we the forerunners in our nation have this distinguished task to do so. If there is anyone in this august gathering that has anything to the contrary let him stand up and say so because our father, brother, the leader is of the sound opinion that total or sweeping consensus is needed to back up his plea…..[eyes the Parliamentarians, especially members from the opposition. By this time fully-armed state security police have had the audacity to brave the doors of the Well of Parliament. They have orders from somewhere to breach the sanctity of Parliament because underground intelligence has suggested that infiltrators have entered the country and are prepared to wreak havoc. This novelty alarms the novitiates and causes their heads to turn to the Honourable Speaker for an explanation]

It is a new security strategy to guarantee our safety we being the foremost citizens after our blessed leader … do you have any dissenting voices to what we are gathered here for? [no one chooses to speak though some do fidget and turn incessantly as if ready to voice off to attract admiration from the audience upstairs. Otherwise silence reigns]

So I take it that even our colleagues from the other side i.e. the glorious opposition approve of what has been tabled before the House?

[The immaculately dressed parliamentarian, some with new bungalows, cars promises of lucrative contracts and other mouth-watering inducements, dreams of wrapping up the proceedings quickly in order to attend to other matters]

Would some Honourable Members move that the Bill be adopted?

Hon. Lonka: [Stands up. Eyes the gathering, trembling and sweat sufficiently large enough running down the middle of his back into his underwear, down his leg, on top of his sock into his shoe] I m-o-v-e that the Bill be a-d-o-p-t-e-d. [Hurriedly sinks into his seat].

Speaker: [Glasses, almost falling off a virtually non-existent nose, hangs reluctantly to his cadaverous face with the help of a thick cord the size of his shoe lace]. Any seconder?

Hon. Juma: [A brightly fair –complexioned frame who is not known to say anything when in Parliament beyond 'I concur', stands up, eyes everyone from behind a pair of clear silver-rimmed glasses, timidly]. I do ... [Disappears into the oblivion of his cushioned seat].

Hon. Speaker: [Gloats by revealing rows of tarred teeth in the middle of which a gulley is uncharacteristically prominent]. I thank you ladies and gentlemen and the State Security Police for a day well spent.

[Wraps the gavel on the table in an undignified manner]

[Light fades]

ACT THREE SCENE 2

CITY

MR. COLE'S RESIDENCE

AFTERNOON

Mr Cole is sprawled on his carpet like a sheep waiting to be slaughtered. His lair is a two-roomed affair with an appendage which he proudly accepts as the service outlet. The chairs in his parlour he has inherited from an uncle with whom he has unclear linage. Cole has been grateful because the photo of the mysterious uncle looms over the door to the bedroom which contains no bed but a coloured mat that has been given to him by an aunt from his maternal side. To the left on entering the parlour from the outside stands a dressing-mirror that has withstood thirteen onslaughts from ravaging insects. Presently the frame of the entire dressing-mirror is facing the fourteenth and might as well be the final attack that will herald its demise to a concluding finale. Cole has little belongings other than his carpet and ghostly dressing-mirror. Otherwise his worldly possession could fit into a black plastic bag. The wife or inmate, Fatalie, is outside by the door in a guise that suggests that she is guarding the entrance to Cole's apartment. The veranda Fatalie is occupying stretches to the left and right sides. Fatalie's palms are propping up her face causing her lips and jaws to metamorphose into each other. Her elbows are supported by her aching knees which are pressing down a pair of gulley-ridden feet that have tramped the unfriendly roads of the city in the hope of finding a customer who would appreciate her rather distasteful façade.

Fatalie: [Desperately] Coleson! Coleson! Please wake up! Won't you please stand up and be a man for just one minute? How do we provide food for Tamatfa? She will return from school very soon and you are yet to get up from there.

Mr Cole: [Grumbling]. The Lord will provide. An entrance is meant to be entered and a mouth is meant to be fed. Why are you worried? You fuss a lot. Do you have some change? [Chuckles to himself]. I know you do. Please get me two sticks of cigarettes and two mints I mean sweets. Ok.

Fatalie: [Angry] Do I chop off your fingers and sell them in order to buy what you've just asked for? ... Let me warn you, the State Security Police will not tolerate any rabble-rousing antic in the name of free speech ... they will arrest and detain without observing the due process of the law.

Cole: [Erect]. Are you one of them? I thought you were one of us. When have they gotten onto you? Last night? You coward!

[Enters Tamatfa]

Tamatfa: [Smiling but hungry]. Mummy, good afternoon! Where is daddy?

Fatalie: [Disturbed]. Good afternoon! How was school today?

Tamatfa [Excited]. Fine ... ehh ... we are going to be fed in school daily.

[Cole stands in the doorway]

Cole: [Confidently]. I did say don't worry. No money before she arrived. Now feeding at school. Good afternoon Tamatfa. More good tidings?

Fatalie: [Gnashing her teeth]. Shameless fool! You allow others to feed your daughter for you!

Tamatfa: [Desperate to reconcile the two]. We are not supposed to pay school fees any longer.

Cole: [Enthusiastically]. Did you hear THAT?

Tamatfa: [Twisting her belly with her right hand]. Mummy I'm hungry!

Fatalie and Cole: [Exchange swift glances and in unison]. Darling, please give us three minutes and you'll have your food. Go in and change into something better. We are taking you out for lunch.

[Tamatfa enters whilst Fatalie and Cole follow from behind]   [Light fades out]
ACT THREE SCENE 3

CITY

AFTERNOON

BAR & RESTAURANT

Paul's Rendez-vous is boiling with activity. It is a bee-hive. Customers are ordering and waiters or attendants are doing endless rounds to and from the kitchen. Overhead, what looks like a ceiling, is a crisscross of thin fibres wired behind overhanging bulbs. These fibres are connected to mostly, dysfunctional extension speakers, acquired through dubious means. The main music source supplying these white elephants is a stolen car-tape that has been given to Paul to offset long overdue outstanding debts. And Paul had threatened fire and brimstone. The debtor not wanting to be seen as defaulting in his obligation made deep run for it by wrenching the car-tape from an unsuspecting car-owner who had parked his car in order to attend a little affair in the red light district frequented by married men. The Afternoon Buzz is anchored by Jay Bee and he punctuates his programme with strong Afro-beats from around the continent and beyond. Once in a while the programme is interrupted by some official announcer from State House and the State Security Police

50

Headquarters. The noises from spoons, forks, knives, plates, and cups are not drowning the livid conversations and the sounds from the ageing speakers.

Fatalie: [Beaming with a mouthful and spoon in full readiness]. A delicious meal!

Tamatfa: [Laughs]. Mummy the food is falling off your mouth!

Cole: [Teasingly]: She promised to out-eat us!

Radio Announcer: Listeners stand by for a press release from State House. The government have viewed with utmost concern the nefarious activities of some misguided individuals within our midst. These activities have been planned by the enemies of our young Republic. These wicked people will not stop at anything in their quest for power. In this light, citizens are warned to be vigilant and must report any untoward activity to the nearest State Security agents. Listeners remain glued to your set for more information on the matter ... Now, ladies and gentlemen a song from Miles Davies...

[Boima enters]

Boima: [Notices the Coles]. A family outing or what?

Tamatfa: [Gleefully]. Uncle Boima, come and join us.

Boima: [Proudly]. A doll for you on your ninth birthday!

Tamatfa: [Almost losing her breath]. Are you serious? Thank you, uncle.

Boima: [Turns to Cole and Fatalie]. I have not received my salary for some months now. I wonder what is happening?

Cole: [Sits upright and closes ranks with Boima]. Don't speak it out so loudly, you might get marked as a sabboteur.

Fatalie: [Emphatically]. Boima I suggest you heed Cole's advice. In fact, let us leave for our respective homes [in a rather hushed tone] I think walls have ears. [Even more quietly] students, I heard, are not happy.

Tamatfa: [Curious]. Share it with me!

Radio Announcer: Listeners we have to break our transmission … over to SSP Headquarters …A group of people has been arrested. They were apprehended on the grounds of State House and other public buildings. They've been found having on their person's maps, binoculars, cartridges, pistols and masks. Their motives are yet to be ascertained. In the light of this event, the leader has ordered a dusk-to-dawn curfew effective two hours from now. I thank you.

[Light fades out]

ACT THREE SCENE 4

CITY

NIGHT

THE KELLEH'S RESIDENCE

An extreme weather on a starless night as a storm rages on and an occasional tongue of lightning splits the sky open. The rain is whipping the roof of the Kelleh's. The cold is numbing and the storm is increasing its velocity and perplexed and overwhelmed vultures are being buffeted here and there in the night sky. In the distance, roofs are being flown off their support frames and the cries of subdued neighbours could be heard faintly but sufficiently to identify their owners. Guest and hosts are huddling in the parlour all cold with hunger and jolted by the lashes of privation and misdirected anger.

Pa Kelleh: [Shamefacedly]. This has never happened in this house!

Borbor Kelleh: [Stretched full on the floor]. Things will get better very soon.

Mama Kelleh: [Retorts hastily]. Keep quiet. You are in the presence of elders.

Mamady: [Yawning].I warned you to stay put but you didn't listen to me.

Pa Morlai: [Eye popping out]. Mama Morlai did you hear what your daughter has said?

Mama Morlai: [Defensively]. She is just a child; she must be ignored.

Borbor Morlai: [Pangs of hunger eating into his intestines thereby increasing his frustration]. I can't stand this anymore. Can't one go out just for a moment?

Borbor Kelleh: [Sarcastically]. Unless, you want to be served daily and on time at a different address …!

Pa Kelleh: [Sternly]. Borbor Morlai, please, sit down. There is a curfew and no one is allowed to go out of his or her house and besides it is raining.

Borbor Morlai: [Desperately]. But I can't die here for want of food when I could get some outside.

Borbor Kelleh: [Stands up and faces his father]. Papa the fees or I don't go to school tomorrow.

Mama Kelleh: [Reassuringly]. You will definitely have it tomorrow or you'll take a letter to the school authorities to allow you for a while…I wonder why this idea of free –education is not working at all…

[Knocking outside]

Who is it?

Bellcamp: [Angrily]. Landlord!

Pa Kelleh [rushes to the door and opens it]. Good evening Mr. Bellcamp.

Bellcamp: [Puffing hard at his pipe and gruffly]. Bad evening to you and your band of city-mongers. My rents!

Mama Kelleh: [Pleadingly]. Please Mr. Landlord Bellcamp, give us some time and don't shame us in front of my relatives. I sh….

Bellcamp: [Stamping his left foot and shaking his overstuffed stomach that is at bursting point as the navel button is off]. No more of this postponing. I have a way out.

Pa Kelleh: [Knocking and holding Bellcamp's left foot and this makes his head invisible to Bellcamp]. What is it sir?

Bellcamp: [Smiles as he notices an opportunity to make an extra profit]. Someone has offered to pay more than you are paying and is willing to boot you out himself and I want to let him …

The Kelleh's and the Morlai's: [In unison]. We shall pay what he has offered you after we would have settled our arrears.

[Lights fade out]

ACT FOUR SCENE 1

MORNING

SCHOOL

The sun is up as usual, airy but not stormy. The silence is the usual one that characterises school compounds all over. Classes are in progress and the principal has just concluded his usual daily early-morning supervision rounds that would guarantee him the opportunity to belittle teachers and pupils who might be slightly off the mark. Its assembly ground is paved and located in the centre and the classrooms are constructed in a circumference manner. The national and school flags dot the mature morning sky as vultures and other birds hover in the sky enough to attract the attention of the free citizens who inhibit the space below. There is a teacher in Borbor Kelleh and Tamatfa's class. The subject is National History and the lesson is on repressive regimes. Mr. Bomti is reading from a textbook which he only could afford. And occasionally quotations will be delivered to the admiration of the pupils.

Mr Bomti: [Holds the textbook in one hand and chalk and paper in the other. His back is to the blackboard as its importance has been secondary. Loudly, he reads]. "The nation has endured so many coups. This sad state of affairs stems from issues of bad governance. This in turn will mature into uncalled for unrests in the guises of demonstrations and the banning of newspapers .... normally when coups are not in the making, leadership

57

tussles will punctuate the political landscape …. the ordinary citizens the victim…"

[Eyes away from book]

Class if I may buttress a bit, our beloved nation has been characterised by chaos because our leaders have ushered in a new era that will rid this nation of party multiplicity. It is sad that some of us have refused to see the well-meaning intentions of our leaders … we are one people so why go under different names … you may agree with my reasoning that the abductions, students' unrests and cannibalisms have stopped completely since the new law came into force … even the mischief-making tabloid no longer controls the mainstream …

[Bell rings Mr Bomti hurries out of class for lunch]

[Tamatfa and Borbor Kelleh are holding hands and looking for their Eden, which is under the shade of an apple tree. Today they are the first and so will monopolize the rendezvous to his hearts' content. Tamatfa has developed into a ripe corn that is unlikely to pass unnoticed; her face has been sculpted to pass for any model. Her lips are thick and her nose is pointed sufficiently enough to misplace are race. Borbor Kelleh has a solid frame but not as tall and graceful like Tamatfa's. Their appearances set them apart. In the blood of Tamatfa runs the life of the newly-rich, a complex in the poor suburbs off the capital with a car for smallest of errands like the purchase of parched peanuts from Mammy Yaba. The chemistry that brings them together has been largely unfathomable]

Tamatfa: [Crisply]. Hurry! Borbor! Hurry! I can't wait to narrate the film we watched last night.

Borbor Kelleh: [Eagerly]. And what about it?

Tamatfa: [Beams]. It is about two lovers from unequal backgrounds and the parents not wanting their union to continue.

Borbor Kelleh: [Sadly]. It's too bad for them. How did they sort it out in the end?

Tamatfa: [Looks into the eyes of Borbor Kelleh]. They both went their separate ways.

Borbor Kelleh: [Sadly]. Another ending could have been better.

[Horn from a distance]

Tamatfa: [Excitedly]. Oh! Borbor wait for me I'll be back in a moment. [Notices the sombre look on Borbor Kelleh's face]. Are you jealous? You funny fool, try and be sensible!

[Runs away]

Borbor Kelleh: [Pensively]. Can I win this battle? The odds are against me. No money, her parents hate my presence like the dog does the cat, my parents are out-matched, out-classed, my friends hopeless ... I might just get lucky.

(Light fades out)

ACT FOUR SCENCE 2

CITY

BORBOR KELLEH'S RESIDENCE

The residence is located in another part of the city suburbs. Borbor Kelleh approaches the door only to be greeted by invectives from his uncle who has come into Borbor Kelleh's mother. She is his latest acquisition after the death of Papa Kelleh. The uncle is only doing him a favour-continuing the family lineage in Papa Kelleh's absence.

Uncle Kelleh: [Sweating profusely and wielding a large stick in his right hand and holding Mama Kelleh with his left hand. Mama Kelleh's hands are on top of her head and her knees slightly bent outwards straining the knee caps]. You idiot! Bed sheet waster! How many times must you fool the Kelleh family? When is it coming? A new member is needed in the family and you can't respond?

[Notices Borbor Kelleh]

...you vermin come this way. Haven't I warned you about coming from school late? You've been with Tamatfa? Eh? She is not for you. Her father is a diamond official – Mines Inspector. Do you understand me? Look for your level. It's only the insane rat that would dare the cat to a duel.

[Turns to Mama Kelleh as he releases his grip on her throat]

Your son has saved you. Now go and prepare the evening meal! This is how you wrecked the life of my elder brother. I'm too strong for you ... by the way when my wife and children return from town serve them and tell them not to wait for me ... [Looks at Borbor Kelleh who is fuming with murderous rage ... [Quietly] just like your relatives that had just deserted you ... [loudly] and you stay away from that filth that you call your honey. Don't bring her father's dirty wealth into this house. Is that clear?

[Disappears]

Borbor Kelleh: [Weakly]. Yes sir! [Rushes to his mother, who by now is a bundle of crumpled sadness and mortification on the floor].

ACT FOUR SCENE 3

CITY

COLE'S RESIDENCE AT NIGHT

The compound is a walled-barbed-wire affair. The huge and solid gate is meant to withstand a grenade attack. Beyond the gate is dotted with cars of every available and expensive make. The house is located further in land behind a long row of tall trees that refuse to give the house away. It is a two-storey apartment that has most of everything on both storeys. Mr Cole is a man of taste and his elegance and riches have defied logic. No one in the neighbourhood knows how he has come into such massive wealth. Rumours are that he is in the diamond business but so are others who are not as rich as he is. His car swings into view with horn blaring causing the midnight calm to crack. As if on impulse the structure behind the trees comes into life as lights begin to go on in every part of the magnificent edifice. He has uniformed guards - three of them and countless other house- helps who come and go as demand requires. He keeps a big kitchen and openly philanders a lot.

Cole: [Jubilantly]. Is anyone in? I'm home! Tamatfa? Fatalie? Where are you?

[They rush downstairs reluctantly from their respective TV rooms]

Fatalie and Tamatfa: [Gleefully]. Welcome home! How was the trip? Did you sell well? Are there new customers?

Cole: [Reaches out for the waistlines of both and squeezes them close to his frame with a devouring embrace]. Everything went as planned. Did not miss flights. Accurate hotel booking! Prompt business transaction, secure transfer, new prospects and guess what?

Fatalie and Tamatfa: [In unison]. Ahh? Ahh?

Cole: [Effusively]. Fantastic sights and acquaintances!

Fatalie: [Suspicious]. And nothing unusual? Eh? Eh?

Cole: [Realises his mistake and then tries to change the subject]. Come of it … ah! ... ah! ... what do you take me for. A rake? ... Tamatfa, that boy of yours, stay away from him!..

Tamatfa: [Mumbling]. Yes, sir!

Fatalie: [Happily]. Please listen to your father!

Cole: [Confidently]. That's my girl [to Fatalie] you know we must be careful of folks around us. They are jealous of our success. And for our little precious girl to fall in love with one of their sons is a bad sign.

Tamatfa: [Grudgingly]. Dad! Please stop. It is not what you think.

Cole: [Visibly angry]. What is it then? Why would a fly hover around a juicy mango? Tell me!

Fatalie: [Anxiously]. Come off it you two. Make up and let us welcome Daddy from a long and successful trip abroad. [Light fades out]

63

ACT FOUR SCENE 4

CITY

JAY'S COMMON HUNT

NIGHT

An odd collection of young misguided perverts gather every day, dawn to dawn, at Jay's Common Hunt. Discussions range from politics to love making. Football arguments form the agenda for the most part of their 'brainstorming' as would-be academic drop outs would put it. Booze, the local brew, cigarettes, marijuana, information about the current pimps will normally pass around unimpeded. They sit in a circle and in the centre a kerosene lamp, actually a fire issuing from an elongated mouth of normal liquid Peak Milk tin. The fire is naked. Jay responded slowly to the frequenters' demands because for them time has to wait. They are not in a hurry. Their marathon conversation drags on lazily, leisurely and hardly attracting any alterations. They are, largely, the peaceful corps. Their source of income is a mystery save for Jay whom they buy from.

Borbor Kelleh: [Trembling from the cold outside]. Jay, a torch please!

Jay: [Guardedly]. Are you loaded to roll?

Borbor Kelleh: [Assumingly]. Do you think otherwise? Here! Now, the torch.

[Jay hands him a small object in the guise of a ball with paper rolled over it]

64

Feroz: [Mumbles]. B K, service to the peaceful corps? One could do man! Please lend a hand!

[Borbor kelleh readily splits his acquisition]

Borbor Kelleh: [Happily]. Here take this! Potato leaf palms.

Feroz: [Concernedly]. Sorry about what happened to your father. Elections in this country are always violent. [Wraps his semi-sling and waits for fire, draws at it and inhales deeply]. Hmm! There is word going round [whispers] that the army is recruiting.

Borbor Kelleh: [Excited]. What is your source?

Feroz: [Enthusiastically]. From the inside [whispers]. The leader wants to pass over the baton and thus deems it wise to have new blood in the national army to foil the aspirations of older contenders

Borbor Kelleh: [Awed]. You appear so wise today!

Feroz: [Expertly]. It's time we join in in order to even up … remember your uncle, Tamatfa's father, the landlord … eh?

[Lights fade out]

ACT FOUR SCENE 5

CITY

MORNING

MARKET

Mama Morlai, Mama Kelleh and Mamady are now selling at the local market though they are living far apart.

Mamady: [Beaming]. Aunty, do you hear from Borbor Kelleh? How is he doing in the National Army?

Mama Kelleh: [sobs]. I don't want to hear about it! I know I'll lose him as I lost his father! B K does not listen to me any longer. He thinks he is man enough to take up soldiering.

[Enters Mama Morlai]

Mama Morlai: [Sternly]. You Mamady you are the one? Eh? Why do you keep opening up old wounds? Don't you know that the size of the elephant is worry sufficient for it?

Mama Kelleh: [Regaining her composure]. It was a genuine question. I will try to get over it. How is my brother? Is he at home?

Mama Morlai: [Guiltily]. He works at Mr. Cole's residence. He does the night shift in addition to guarding the daughter. Tamatfa.

Mama Kelleh: [Remembers]. Eh! Eh! Someone told me that there is ... [Moves closer to Mama Morlai] fighting from where your people hail from?

Mamady: [Curious]. Are you sure?

Mama Kelleh: [Confidently]. As daylight! They bring the wounded from there on a daily basis [a siren is heard from a muddied military ambulance that zooms past them].

Mama Morlai: [Fearfully]. It might be getting worse! By the way who is fighting who?

Mama Kelleh: [Whispers]: People who are not satisfied with the present status quo and the National Army [sobs] and my son is to be sent there.

Mamady: [Prodding]. Are they going to be deployed this soonest? Stay calm!

Mama Kelleh: [Raises both arms to the sky with face upward]. Protect him and protect me from my new husband and team.

[Customer calls].

ACT FIVE SCENE 1

RURAL HEADQUARTER

RURAL SURBURBS

AFTERNOON

The overthrow of the leader's regime is followed by panic in the land and especially, the rural suburbs. It is the birth-place of Boima the ex-government functionary. He is on a forced voluntary retirement and has opted to while away the time in his homeland among his paternal relatives. It is a sunny afternoon and the weekend market is in full swing. Goods have been brought from the most northern parts of the land for sale in Boima's homeland. There are people from distant lands whose wares include gorgeous ornaments like trinkets, chains, rings and ear-rings. Kola is in abundance together with exotic fabric from the eastern parts of the country. The rural residents are out in their best weekend-market suits with the local currency fighting to get out of their hiding places. The wind is friendly and the afternoon sky's traffic is busy as eager vultures and other birds hover above.

Boima: [Approaches a stranger]. Are you from here?
Stranger: [Surprised]. No! Why?
Boima: [Conciliatory]. You resemble a colleague of mine from a distant part of our land.
Stranger: [Relieved] Ah! Are you a native?
Boima: [Proudly]. Yes, of course!

Stranger: [Countenance changes]. You are proud of your lineage as I can see from the energy you've marshalled to pronounce your attachment.

Boima: [Smiles]. And … you are from where?

Stranger: [Confidently]. From some other parts, I'm here to see the nature of trade in these parts.

Boima: [Enquiringly]. Staying for too long?

Stranger: [Affirmatively]. Brief. But might be dramatic!

Boima: [Suspicious]. Why dramatic?

Stranger: [Looks around]. We're cutting off this part from the central authorities' reach … [disappears quickly as it begins to rain heavily followed by huge thunderclaps and blinding lightning flashes]

Boima [speechless] oh! Oh! …

[Lights fade out…]

ACT FIVE SCENE 2

CITY SURBURBS

On a road in the suburbs, Borbor Kelleh clad in military fatigue, having just gone through the passing-out ceremonies, is plodding his way home. His boots are hosting the remainder of his trousers. A belt is responsible for the prominence of his thin waistline. His back and shoulders are being tormented by a heavy sack whose top is almost chopping off the back of his head that is hidden under a metal helmet which is also causing considerable irritation to the underside of his chin, jaws and ears as a result of cord that links all these body-parts in one fell swoop. Kelleh's chest and stomach are stuffed to the point that one would think of him as ready to swim. Kelleh is romping home triumphantly and prays to happen on Tamatfa. She, coincidentally, is coming from the opposite direction.

Borbor Kelleh: [Notices Tamatfa and decides to readjust his gait]. What am I seeing? [Quietly to himself].

Tamatfa: [Notices the uniform figure and flinches]. I hate them! [Muses to herself].

Borbor Kelleh: [Closes in on her]. Hi won't you look at me please.

Tamatfa: [Realises her mistake]. Is it you? BK! [She hugs him and showers kisses on him and Kelleh blushes].

Borbor Kelleh: [Regaining control of himself]. Control yourself! I am a soldier now. You are displaying excessive emotion which is bad for someone like me.

Tamatfa: [Ignores the reprimand]: Why didn't you tell me you were joining the army?

Borbor Kelleh: [More masculine]: It's a man thing. Women must be surprised thus they should not form part of the planning process. You would have advised me otherwise which would have been unpatriotic.

Tamatfa: [Crying]. Do I mean something to you?

Borbor Kelleh: [Bluffing]. Then ...

Tamatfa: [Fighting back]. And now?

Borbor Kelleh: [Conquering]. Might not be quite.

Tamatfa: [Refusing to give in]. I'm sorry for my parents' behaviour. You know I love you.

Borbor Kelleh: [Beginning to hate himself]. Let me see you home [Holding her hand].

Tamatfa: [Head on Kelleh's shoulder and their hands on each other's waistline]. Does the National Army teach you to forget you first love?

Borbor Kelleh: [Smiles]. Quite the reverse!

[The sun has moved behind them as they approach the shade of a huge palm tree]

ACT FIVE SCENE 3

RURAL SURBURBS

Borbor Kelleh and Feroz are in a camp close to the national borders. The infiltrators occasionally, cross the demarcation line, cause havoc and then retreat into their territories across the separating line. Borbor Kelleh's unit is charged with the task of cutting the rear flanks of the infiltrators when they have breached the legal limits. Borbor Kelleh and Feroz are neck deep in a trench eyes straining underneath camouflage helmets. It is pouring heavily and painfully cold and they are hungry. They dream about finishing up their exercise so that they can join the fleet of their idling numbers in the big towns. Waiting and waiting for what seems to be an eternity is gnawing. Their trained but now tired eyes and fingers are giving away.

Feroz: [Whispering]. We should have been relieved by now.

Borbor Kelleh: [Putting on a brave face]. This is what serving means. Serving without being relieved is part of the training ... stop worrying!

Feroz: [Chuckles]. Look who is talking! Are you not tired of this humdrum?

Borbor Kelleh: [Feigning]. In whose plateau were you trained?

Feroz: [Proudly]. 3624 platoon!

Borbor Kelleh: [Lisping]. No wonder you are chickening! I was in the 21st Century Division.

Feroz [Laughs]. It's no surprise you are not of our time.

[Distant explosion … Boom! Boom!]

[They refocus on their targets i.e. the line …]

Borbor Kelleh: [Almost weeping]. It's becoming nasty.

Feroz: [Mockingly]. I thought you were Rambo or Charles Bronson or Chuck Norris!

Borbor Kelleh: [Weeping]. I miss home. I miss Tamatfa and I hate the infiltrators.

Feroz: [Places a hand on Kelleh's helmet]. Be a man. Let's brave it out. If we are not relieved, we use our prerogative o.k.

Borbor Kelleh: [Nods as his nose starts running]. Do …. [Hears a sound] listen!

Feroz: [Stiffens his ears but hears nothing]. What is it?

Borbor Kelleh: [Realises his foolishness]. It's my gambling dices!

[Darkness descends on them and it continues to pour]

ACT FIVE SCENE 4

CITY

NIGHT

Borbor Kelleh and Tamatfa are seated in their parlour and on the floor Junior Kelleh is tramping on all four upsetting whatever is within sight and reach to the laughter and consternation of both parents. The parlour has the rich trappings of Tamatfa's parents' home. On the wooden stand is a clock that chimes lazily. Not far from Borbor Kelleh's head is the radio blasting off in all its zeal as it is finding it difficult to fit in this new environment after been wrenched violently from the rural suburbs. Kelleh's right hand bandaged right up to the shoulders. A bullet mark is glazed on his left buttock.

Borbor Kelleh: [Groans]. Tam ... Help me stand up!

Tamatfa: [Grumbling]. Borbor Kelleh those pains are not as severe as you think. Feroz took more than your fair share and he is up and running ... I can't put up with this house-help-running-maid antics any longer oh!

Borbor Kelleh: [Looks at her wide-eyed]. Where is your heart? Tell me Tam!

[Junior Kelleh cries]

Tamatfa: [Exasperated]. And now this, as well.

Borbor Kelleh: [Impatiently]. Stop this grumbling. You want to quit? Quit! Ah!

Tamatfa: [Turns violently to face him]. I'm quitting now and I'm going to my father's house. Take care of your handiwork. I should've known. [Runs out of the house]

Borbor Kelleh: [Realising his mistake]. I was just joking. Please come back if not for me but for Junior … please … [Sobs].

Radio: Listeners this is an important press release from State House … 'The newly-elected government of … [baby cries] has been overthrown and the infiltrators who have been fighting in the suburbs of the rural areas have been called to the big city to come and take part in the new dispensation. …. [baby cries out louder]… not again … Tamatfa gone, and now this … pointing to the radio and then picking up the child …] … come your father will not forsake you. She will come to her senses one day. [Shooting begins from a far and draws closer to Borbor Kelleh's residence]

ACT FIVE SCENE 5

CITY

MORNING

Borbor Kelleh and Mama Kelleh are seated outside under a tree discussing the fate of Borbor Morlai. It is a sunny morning and a zephyr is caressing the leaves of the mango-tree. Outside the compound is not visible save for the limited view that they get through the wooden entrance whose door has been carted away when the madness was about to end.

Mama Kelleh: [Weeping]. Borbor Morlai is no more. I don't know what got him to join the infiltrators.

Borbor Kelleh: [Looking outside expectedly]. Mama it's enough …. haven't you seen Junior? It is past time now. Is he waiting for afternoon classes?

Mama Kelleh: [Raising her head]. Are you not concerned about your late cousin?

Borbor Kelleh: [Reassuringly]. I do but we have the living to look after as well.

Mama Kelleh: [Hesitates]. Have you heard from Tamatfa? Is she coming back?

Borbor Kelleh: [Evasive]. She knows where I am!

Mama Kelleh: [Changes the subject]. Mamady is coming to stay with us for the weekend. Are you looking forward to seeing her?

Borbor Kelleh: [Still looking at the entrance]. If she does not over stay! …

Vendor: [Eagerly]. The Dailies! The Dailies!

Borbor Kelly: [Excitedly] Eh......paper man come this way. [Vendor enters]. What do we have here? "Supplies meant for vulnerable find their way to the market stalls". "State officials get expensive four-wheel drives for official duty". "Leader contemplates term-limit extension".

Vendor: [Angry]. Which one do you want sir?

Borbor Kelleh: [Skims the other paper]. "Infiltrators, coupists and the re-instated collaborate".

Vendor: [Exasperatedly]. Mister leave my papers ... you know you are not buying ... [wrenches papers from Kelleh's hand and rushes out].

Borbor Kelleh: [Laughs]. Wait! Guess this means mending fences"... [Burst out laughing]

Junior Kelly: [Laughing]. Papa! Papa!

Borbor kelleh [hugs junior]. My champion! ... [Light fades out].

ACT SIX SCENE 1

ABROAD

NIGHT

This is Tamatfa's one-room apartment in the busiest district of an affluent settlement. The skies are dark but the magnificent lighting system makes up for the gloominess of the firmament. Snaky streets as wide as the ocean floor assert themselves majestically on the burgeoning expanse of blocks that have become the settlement's landmarks. Beckoning messages in brilliant displays assault the eye at every given opportunity. These lights and advertisements hardly miss their targets. The citizens are forever running to catch up with nightmarish deadliness on every luxury that has been offered them. It is pouring slightly and the fog has cleared a bit but not without the propensity to blur the exhausted pedestrian on his way home from forced or voluntary slavery.

Tamatfa: [Approaching the porter]. Evening!
Porter: [Hands in pockets and chin, mouth submerged in the lapels of an oversized coat]. Evening mam! ....
[Hands her the keys] …. have a nice sleep!
Tamatfa: [Admires the punctuality of the doorman]. You are always on time.
Porter: [Chuckles]. I have to because my college career depends on it!
Tamatfa: [Generously hands him money]. Would you mind?

Porter: [Embarrassed]. Yes I do … keep it …. This is the land of milk and honey!

Tamatfa: [Hurt]. Sorry … [Rushes up the stairs to her flat's door. Turns the key, closes the door behind her and stretches full length on her bed and sleeps fitfully].

Tamatfa Dreams …

Restaurant Boss: Hey! You! …. Serve those customers quickly … are you dreaming?

Tamatfa: [Angry]. No!

Restaurant Boss: [Grates his teeth]. Then shake off your slumber and make money for this joint or you start looking for another job.

Tamatfa: [Exasperated]. No free things here [She admits to herself quietly as she rushes to and from the kitchen with an alacrity that frightens her … I wish I could see my son and …

Restaurant Boss: [Fuming]. Get going.

Tamatfa: [Responding even more vigorously] it's alright, O.K.?

Customers' Voices: [Randomly]. Waiter, food, waiter ….food … attendant …. Mummy.

Tamatfa: [Wakes up and puts on the TV]. Ah! … This is not home! …I can't cope with a torn mind …. [Switches TV off]

[Lights fade out]

ACT SIX SCENE 2

CITY

MORNING

Borbor Kelleh, Mama Kelleh and Mamady are under the yard tree awaiting the arrival of Papa and Mama Morlai. The monopolisers of the skies are out in their usual exuberance occasionally greeting their opposite numbers who are seated under the tree with cries and excrements. The latter will provoke instantaneous head turning upward to punish the doers with eyes that could have shot arrows after them. This does not happen for humans have their limitations. It rained last night as the ground is wet and soft. The dust smell becomes pervasive and tantalizing as it mingles with the scent of rawness from the leaves in and around the yard. Junior is at Sunday School.

Papa Morlai and Mama Morlai: [Following after the other rush through the gate and deliver a unitary greeting]. Good morning!

Borbor Kelleh, Mama Kelleh and Mamady: [In unison]. Good morning!

Papa Morlai: [Looks at Mama Kelleh]. I think it's good we return to the countryside since the turbulence has subsided.

Mama Kelleh: [Surprised]. Why the sudden change of heart?

Mama Morlai: [Bowing]. We are better off over there ... you know what I mean ... there is the farm, the poultry and the house to look after.

Borbor Kelleh: [Speechless]. If you insist ... when are you leaving?

Papa Morlai: [Confidently]. Tomorrow .... Mamady are you going back?

Mamady: [Proudly]. Of course papa! You know I love the countryside.

Mama Kelleh: [Eyes lit up]. But you'll not forget us brother, eh?

Papa Morlai: [Embraces his sister]. You are always my little one and I shall always protect you. Just call me in your dreams and I will just happen at your door step.

Borbor Kelleh: [Stands up, looks into the sky, turns to the gate and looks at his people]. Let's go inside and have some breakfast ... a successful day begins with a filled stomach ...

Junior Kelleh: [At the gate]. Papa, aunty, grandpa and grandma! [They all turn to look at who is calling after them].

All: [Ecstatically]. So it's you! ... You! ....You! Little champion! Come in. [They gather around him and lift him up to the sky ...]

[Door closes].

ACT SIX SCENE 3

EVENING

CITY

Tamatfa enters the gate of Borbor Kelleh. She is rattled but ready to own up and make up. She is holding bags on both hands and another slung over her shoulder. Her pair of trousers is oversized on top of which is a jeans jacket. She has a pair of glasses on her forehead. The lips are reddened and the earrings are hanging proudly on either ear. A chain is tightened around her neck and another of similar make is chained to her left hand on top of which is a masculine watch. The fingers are unburdened though the nose has not been spared. She stands just outside the gateless entrance ... Waiting .....
Confused!

Junior Kelleh: [Comes to the veranda and sees the figure and gets curious]. Eh! What are you doing there? Are you looking for someone?

Voices: [From within]. What is it junior?

Junior: [Raises his voice]. Someone is standing at the gate and refuses to go away.

[All come to the veranda. They see her figure but are unable to recognise her. Mama Kelleh and Borbor Kelleh take a closer look and Papa Morlai also responds likewise.

Tamatfa: [Eyes watering]. I-t-'s .... m-e .... T-a-m-a-t-f-a ....! [Weeps openly and is about to fall to the ground ...

they all but Borbor Kelleh rush to prevent her from reaching the floor down].

All: [Eagerly]. Hold it! Hold it! You've come a long way! ... We love you!

Tamatfa: [In Mama Kelleh's arms]. I'm sorry .... I was foolish and spoilt ... wet in the ears [Looks for Borbor Kelleh and Junior Kelleh].

Borbor Kelleh and Junior ... [Standing by each other weeping]. We know... life is the best teacher.... come and be for we are ...

[Spread out their arms as they move towards her. Tamatfa weeps uncontrollably hugging Junior with one hand and the other hand limping freely]. Junior I've been foolish.....please forgive me.

Junior: [Looks into her eyes and wipes her tears with his right hand]. I love you mother ... Come on... [He turns to Borbor Kelleh]... Papa, take her hand ... [Borbor Kelleh weeps freely while the others watch]

[Lights fade out].

ACT SIX SCENE 4

AFTERNOON

FOOTBALL MATCH

The Reunion Stadium is filled to capacity. Everyone is clad in their best outdoor dress. Some parents have their kids seated by their sides. Others mount their children high up in order to guarantee them a spectacular view of the match in progress. Junior is seating on his father's shoulders and Tamatfa, now pregnant, is holding on to Borbor Kelleh's left hand as if the hand means the world to her - it sure is. Junior is having a lollipop in one hand and the other hand is clasped round the upper parts of his father's head. The visiting national team are having a fair advantage over the home-team whose supporters are crying their throats hoarse in order to rally them forward. The skies are brilliant and are dotted with vultures and other birds hovering above hoping to benefit from the left overs of their human counterparts in the stands below.

Borbor Kelleh: [Concerned]. What is wrong with our left back, eh? Hasn't he eaten this morning?

Junior Kelleh: [Laughs]. He did papa. Both of us ate together this morning. He is just lazy.

Tamatfa: [Unmindful of the match]. Why can't we take a stroll outside? I'm tired of this tedium.

Borbor Kelleh: [Supportively]. You are right! Let's go somewhere. Maybe she is .... [Points at the pregnancy]... jealous or wants to say something.

Junior Kelleh: [Curious]. Who are you talking about?

Tamatfa: [Looks at Junior]. Your sister!

Junior Kelleh: [Jealous]. I've no sister!

Borbor Kelleh: [Coaxingly]. You'll have and I guess you need someone to bully and protect.

Junior Kelleh: [Laughs]. I'll rather protect her.

Borbor Kelleh puts Junior down and uses both arms to steady his charges protectively.

[They go outside onto the terrace of Reunion Stadium. From inside the stands, the frustrations, urgings and cheering go on as the sun settles behind the palm tree leaves to prepare for another day. Up in the sky, the vultures and other birds are disappearing further into the horizon]. **[Curtains fall]**

SIERRA LEONEAN WRITERS SERIES (SLWS)

Focusing on academic, fictional, and scientific writing that will complement other relevant materials used in schools, colleges, universities and other tertiary institutions, the Sierra Leonean Writers Series (SLWS) aims to promote good quality books by Sierra Leoneans writing on any topics and other writers from around the world who write on themes and issues about Sierra Leone.

It is the publisher's hope that students and other readers in Sierra Leone will eventually be at least some of the primary beneficiaries of these works. Not only will people in Sierra Leone be able to read materials that relate to their own lives and experiences, budding writers will also be able to draw inspiration from the efforts of their compatriots and other established writers.

Submitted work undergoes a rigorous peer-review process before being accepted for publication, with an international editorial board providing guidance to writers.

SLWS, based in Warima and Freetown in Sierra Leone, distributes books globally through AMAZON.COM. In Sierra Leone, SLWS books are currently available at the SLWS Bookshop in Warima (near Masiaka) and at CLC Bookshop, 92 Pademba Road in Freetown.

SLWS co-publishes some titles with Karantha Publishers in Sierra Leone.

For further information, please visit our website: www.sl-writers-series.org
or contact the publisher, Prof. Osman A. Sankoh (Mallam O.) publisher@sl-writers-series.org

Published Books – a milestone of the 50th title has been reached in September 2016!

1	Osman A. Sankoh (Mallam O.)	2001/ 2016	*A Memoir*	*Hybrid Eyes – An African in Europe*
2	Osman A. Sankoh (Mallam O.)	2001	*Non-fiction*	*Beautiful Colours*
3	Sheikh Umarr Kamarah	2002/ 2015	*Poems*	*Singing in Exile and The Child of War*
4	Abdul B. Kamara	2003/ 2015	*A Memoir*	*Unknown Destination*
5	Samuel Hinton	2003	*Poems*	*The Road to Kenema*
6	Karamoh Kabba	2005/ 2016	*A Novel*	*Morquee – The Political Drama of Wish over Wisdom*
7	Yema Lucilda Hunter	2007	*A Novel*	*Redemption Song*
8	Joe A. D. Alie	2007/ 2015	*Research Text*	*Sierra Leone Since Independence – History of a Postcolonial State*
9	Mohamed Combo Kamanda	2007	*A Play*	*The Visa*
10	J Sorie Conteh	2007	*A Novel*	*In Search of Sons*
11	Michael Fayia Kallon	2010/ 2015	*A Novel*	*The Ghosts of Ngaingah*

12	J Sorie Conteh	2011	*A Novel*	*Family Affairs*
13	Winston Forde	2011	*A Play*	*Layila, Kakatua wan bi Lida*
14	Eustace Palmer Doc P.	2012	*A Novel*	*A Pillar of the Community*
15	Siaka Kroma	2012	*Non-fiction*	*Manners Maketh Man – Adventures of a Bo School Boy*
16	Mohamed Combo Kamanda (ed)	2012	*Short Stories*	*The Price and other Short Stories from Sierra Leone*
17	Sigismond Tucker	2013	*A Memoir*	*From the Land of Diamonds to the Isle of Spice*
18	Bailah Leigh	2013	*Non-fiction*	*Dilemma of Freedom – A Diary from Behind Rebels Lines in the Sierra Leone Civil War*
19	Nnamdi Carew	2013	*A Novella*	*Tiger Fist – Two Stories*
20	Yema Lucilda Hunter	2013	*A Novel*	*Joy Came in the Morning*
21	Ebenezer 'Solo' Collier	2013	*Research Text*	*Primary & Secondary Education in Sierra Leone – Evaluation of more than 50 years of*

				PRACTICES & POLICIES
22	Gbananom Hallowell	2013	*Short Stories*	*Gbomgbosoro - Two Stories*
23	Sheikh Umarr Kamarah & Majorie Jones (eds)	2013	**Poems**	**beg sol noba kuk sup** - *An Anthology of Krio Poetry*
24	Siaka Kroma	2014	*Short Stories*	*Tales from the Fireside*
25	Syl Cheney-Coker*	2014	*Poems*	*The Road to Jamaica*
26	Dr Sama Banya	2015	*A Memoir*	*Looking Back – My Life and Times*
27	Andrew K Keili	2015	*Social Commentary*	*Ponder My Thoughts – Vol. 1*
28	Jedidah A. O. Johnson	2015	*A Novel*	*Youthful Yearnings*
29	Oumar Farouk Sesay	2015	*A Novel*	*Landscape of Memories*
30	Oumar Farouk Sesay	2015	*Poems*	*The Edge of a Cry*
31	Gbanabom Hallowell	2015	*A Novel*	*The Road to Kaibara*
32	Mohamed Gibril Sesay*	2015	*A Novel*	*This Side of Nothingness*
33	Yema Lucilda Hunter	2015	*A Novel*	*Nanna*
34	Yusuf	2015	*Research*	*Development,*

	Bangura		*Text*	*Democracy & Cohesion*
35	Lansana Gberie	2015	*Research Text*	*War, Politics & Justice in West Africa*
36	Yema Lucilda Hunter	2015	*A Biography*	*An African Treasure: In Search of Gladys Casely-Hayford 1904-1950*
37	Moses Kainwo	2015	*Poems*	*Ayo Ayo Ayo and other Love Songs*
38	Abdulai Walon-Jalloh	2015	*Poems*	*Voices and Passions*
39	Gbanabom Hallowell (Ed.)	2016	*Short Stories*	*In the Belly of the Lion – An Anthology of new Sierra Leonean Short Stories*
40	Ahmed Koroma	2016	*Poems*	*Along the Odokoko River - Poems*
41	George Coleridge-Taylor	2016	*A Memoir*	*Transformation in Transition*
42	Karamoh Kabba	2016	*Research Text*	*Fire from Timbuktu: A Dialogue with History*
43	Umu Kultumie Tejan-Jalloh	2016	*A Memoir*	*Telling It As It Was: The Career of A Sierra Leonean Woman in Public Service*

44	Ambrose Massaquoi	2016	*Poems*	*Along the Peal of Drums: Collected Poems (1990-2015)*
45	Mohamed Gibril Sesay	2016	*Poems*	*At the Gathering of Roads (Poems)*
46	Gbanabom Hallowell	2016	*Poems*	*Manscape in the Sierra: New and Collected Poems 1991-2011*
47	Gbanabom Hallowell (Ed.)	2016	*Short Stories and Poems*	*Leoneanthology: Comtemporary Short Stories and Poems from Sierra Leone*
48	Gbanabom Hallowell	2016	*Poems*	*Don't Call Me Elvis and Other Poems*
49	Bakar Mansaray	2016	*Short Stories*	*A Suitcase Full of Dried Fish and Other Stories*
50	Gbanabom Hallowell	2016	*Poems*	*The Art of the Lonely Wanderer*

*co-published with Karantha Publishers

VOICES & PASSIONS

Abdulai Walon-Jalloh

SLWS

VOICES AND PASSIONS

INTRODUCTION

In the past, Sierra Leonean literary writers had struggled for survival especially in the light of other countries whose literature had been very prolific and widely read by a good number of their indigenes and foreigners. Among the protracted challenges associated with that struggle were only few Sierra Leoneans were interested in writing and there was the lack of the necessary impetus. Even when those literary pieces were published, there was no ready market for them to be sold as Sierra Leoneans then preferred reading literature from other countries.

However, at the dawn of the 21st Century, the paradigm shifted and that saw the rise of younger Sierra Leonean writers who were very much desperate to make Sierra Leonean Literature not only widespread in the country but also transcend borders. This new wave brought about a proliferation of the three literary genres by Sierra Leonean writers.

The University of Sierra Leone was not complacent about the new wave and lecturers, who are talented in writing, joined the blaze as they too wanted to share their remarkable experiences with those near and far.

The present collection is the maiden edition of a thorough and focused work of one of the lecturers in the

Language Studies Department at Fourah Bay College – University of Sierra Leone.

Simply written, the poet brings out a good number of experiences (both personal and general) which are highly descriptive, thus making them very compelling to readers. These past, present and future issues described are neatly woven in the different lines and stanzas of the collection which ultimately makes it one of high quality in Sierra Leonean poetry.

With a variety of rhythm and number of lines per stanza, the poet equally makes use of the different literary devices in order to make the reader thrilled from start to finish.

This collection is very much inspirational and as the reader flicks through its rich content, s/he may likely situate him/herself in one or many of the incidents mentioned or even recall remarkable events and places which include 4.27.61 and Kissy Brook.

Prince H. Kenny
Head of Department, Language Studies
Fourah Bay College
University Sierra Leone
July 2015

ENDORSEMENTS

Abdulai Walon-Jalloh's **Voices and Passions** brings us face to face with a poet who is concerned not only with what touches him personally, but also with issues that transcend race, frontier or sex: love, religion, happiness, corruption, politics and nature. We go on a journey with Walon-Jalloh In his debut collection of poetry, as his mind traverses over the places that have moulded his character and left an indelible imprint on his mind; The Sierra Leone Library Board, Kissy Brook, Fourah Bay College and Freetown. The most striking note of his verse is one of restraint, endowed on his poems not only by the matter-of-fact tone in which they are couched, but also in his delight in rhyme. The language of his poems is economical and the haunting beauty or tenderness of a handful of his poems is balm to our souls. His enduring love for Sierra Leone seeps through the pores of his verse and we leave his poems firmly convinced that this volume of poetry is a precursor to other volumes. Like John the Baptist, this volume is sent to prepare the way.

Elizabeth Lucy Kamara
Lecturer of English and Literature
Head of English Language Unit
Fourah Bay College, University of Sierra Leone.

In this haunting collection, Walon-Jalloh's pen comes alive. His themes ranging from the materialism and immorality which are the generic banes of modern societies, to yuletide, the beautiful sterility of Freetown, the birth pangs of nationhood, the differed dream of the Athens of West Africa, the ghastly cadavers that speak of man's propensity to do violence to his brother, the joys of motherhood, the loss of identity and the innocence of childhood encapsulate his inner psychological trauma informed by a desire to find an outlet for long bottled up anger. In the midst of this stanzaic trauma, he pursues his subject matter with an ease and craftsmanship that only a deft artist can. Kafkaesque but mundane, his adroitness with words holds the reader's breath as he explores with poignant frankness his firsthand experience of life in his native Freetown, the poignant beauty of his motherland and the joys of sorrows of his ill-fated compatriots. In this work his themes are as blistering and as variegated as the rawness with which he scythes his experiences. A word economist, Walon-Jalloh's work is an exercise in thematic variance that is the perfect initiation for those who crave after the terrible beauty written with the cadence of verse. **Voices and Passions** is a powerful debut that heralds the dawn of a career that will sparkle for many years to come.

Sheik Bakarr Kamara
Lecturer of Poetry and English
English Language Unit,
Department of Language Studies,
Fourah Bay College, University of Sierra Leone.

Poems in *Voices and Passions*

It's in your Eyes
The East-end
Market Borbor
Congo Dust
Sierra Leone at 48
Freetown Night
The wild
Moments of Glory
The distance
The Story of Life
Living Reality
The Road
Last Line of Defence
Dance in the forests
The Race
The Real Us
The Era of Men
The Baboon's Bottom
Sons of yester years
Happiness
Youths
Success
Where have they gone to?
The Fading

www.ingramcontent.com/pod-product-compliance
Lightning Source LLC
Chambersburg PA
CBHW032004060426
42449CB00031B/404